HOPE FULFILLED

HOPE FULFILLED

*Finding love,
God's way*

PS. ENOCH LAVENDER

Sarah Lavender

Olive Tree Ministries

"*Hope Fulfilled: Finding love, God's way* is the simple yet beautifully told faith story of Enoch and Sarah. Their honesty and disclosure about being promised by God to be married, and then waiting years for it to come to pass, will find an echo with many. Yet, when God moved, things happened at dizzying speed. Within two years, they went from being single to a family of four! The book is transparent, heartfelt, practical and encouraging. If you are waiting, or know someone who is, do yourself a favour and read *Hope Fulfilled*."

Rev. Kameel Majdali, PhD
Director, Teach All Nations

"I am very happy to endorse the message of this book and the wonderful testimonies of Enoch and Sarah on obedience and waiting to hear from God, despite setbacks and disappointments, as they searched for God's will for their marriage partner. I highly recommend this book for anyone who is looking for godly guidelines on how to know if it is God's will to marry, how to find the right partner and how to face pressures and tests during marriage."

Alex Genovese
Director, Derek Prince Ministries-Australia

"Many of us make our decisions, formulate our plans, and then ask God for His blessing. This young couple, Enoch and Sarah, have instead determined to seek the perfect will of God for their lives and consequently, as you will see, He directs their paths (according to Prov. 3:5-6). I commend this spiritual saga, but suggest you read it prayerfully, expectantly, for what He has done for others, He can also do for you!"

Ps Tony Hallo
Townsville, Australia

"*Hope Fulfilled: Finding love, God's way* may bring you to tears as it did for me. It is a touching story of a young man and woman who went through heartache, disappointment and setbacks but held onto God's promise that He would bring them the right marriage partner. The advice they give of holding onto God's promises, though unfulfilled for many years, makes it a book you need to read."

Barbara Miller
Pastor and Author,
Centre for International Reconciliation and Peace

"*Hope Fulfilled: Finding love, God's way* contains the meaningful and moving testimony of the journey of Enoch and Sara Lavender toward achieving a happy Christian marriage. The honest depictions of the challenges, struggles and disappointments they faced, as God prepared them for life together, will inspire others. Enoch and Sarah's experience demonstrates clearly the uniqueness of each marriage journey when God is honoured. His careful, loving guidance shines through these pages that, hopefully, will encourage others to discover their God-given life companion. Their insights are relevant; their experiences often poignant; their lessons timely."

Ps Chris & Ps Erica Grace
Foundations for the Family Ministry

Copyright © 2021 by Ps Enoch Lavender and Sarah Lavender

All rights reserved. No part of this book may be reproduced in any manner whatsoever without written permission except in the case of brief quotations embodied in critical articles and reviews.

ISBN 978-0-6450930-0-1

Unless otherwise indicated, Scripture taken from the New King James Version. Copyright © 1982 by Thomas Nelson, Inc. Used by permission. All rights reserved.

First Printing, 2021

*To those who are waiting for the fulfilment
of a promise from God,
we know and understand that your journey
may have been challenging.
But we want you to know that God
is faithful to keep His promises.*

*In loving memory of Sarah's parents,
Tony and Ngaire French.*

Acknowledgements:

With special thanks to my beloved wife, Sarah, for saying "yes" to God and His plans for her life.

To those who have prayed for, encouraged and counselled us in our respective journeys of waiting for God's promises to be fulfilled.

And a special thanks to our editor and proof reader, Heather King, who helped us get this book to print in record time.

Contents

Introduction   xiii

1. Preparing for the Promise   1
2. A Chance Encounter   10
3. From Heartache to Promise   17
4. Hope Fulfilled   31
5. Are you Waiting for a Promise to be Fulfilled?   39
6. A Fairy Tale Ending   45
7. The Big Picture: Messiah and His Bride   52

Selected Bibliography   66

Recommended Reading   68

Other Books by the Author   71

Introduction

Dear reader,

In this book, Sarah and I want to share with you how God brought us together in marriage. We both had clear promises from God about our future long before we ever met, yet our journey to seeing these promises realised was, at times, frustratingly long and challenging.

One truth we have learnt along the way is that from Heaven's perspective, the journey to the fulfilment of a promise is equally as important as the destination. As the late Bible Teacher Derek Prince once said, "If you are in a hurry to get married, my question to you would be – 'why?'"

We know that we are not the only ones who have been waiting for the fulfilment of promises from God. So if you find yourself now on a similar journey, then this book is for you. We would encourage you not to seek to shortcut God's journey of preparation in your life, but rather allow Him to complete His work in you and lead you into His 'promised land' in His perfect time and way.

Ultimately, our goal of sharing our story is to equip you with some of the life-changing lessons we learnt along the way. We would like to encourage you to trust that God is indeed faithful;

that He hasn't forgotten His promise to you; and that He will bring it to pass when He knows that you are ready.

At the end of this book, we will also share with you some insights into God's intended design for marriage. We will also explore how the Bible's message of Jesus' return to Earth in the End Times is entwined with ancient Jewish wedding customs. And we will show how this relates to us as we live our lives today.

Love and blessings,
Sarah and Enoch,
Melbourne, Australia.

1

Preparing for the Promise

(Enoch writes): I was absolutely stunned by what had just happened. Looking down at the tattered piece of note paper in my hand, I knew more than ever before that God had heard my prayer, and that I had finally met the woman God had chosen for me. God had truly just done an amazing miracle in my life. But before I tell you more of that story, let me first take you back to the very beginning of my journey towards marriage.

An Unexpected Promise

It all started one night in an evening church service in Melbourne back in 2004. Calming piano music filled the auditorium as the Pastor wrapped up his message by asking all of us to quieten our hearts and allow the Holy Spirit to speak to us.

Doing as instructed, I closed my eyes and calmly asked Him to speak to me.

Unexpectedly, I heard the Holy Spirit's quiet and unmistakable whisper in my heart saying, "Are you ready for marriage?" I sat for a while in stunned silence to process what I had just heard.

Being a 20 year-old single male, I certainly was interested in the opposite sex. But getting married anytime soon was definitely not on my radar.

I took a deep breath, considering how to reply. Praying quietly, I responded, "Okay, Lord, but I need you to prepare me."

I optimistically assumed that I would meet Miss Right in a matter of days. After all, it wouldn't take long for Him to prepare me, would it? And if He were speaking about it now, surely it was just about to happen?

Although I realised that I needed preparation, I was yet to find out how much preparation God would have in mind. Little did I know that I was only just embarking on a journey, which would be full of twists and turns and highs and lows, as God began to prepare me to receive the fulfilment of His promise in my life.

The Journey Begins

Expecting Miss Right to show up at anytime, I kept my eyes keenly peeled. "Who is it that God is bringing across my path?" I wondered.

I made a few new friends around this time and decided to zero in on one particular girl in this new circle of friends.

Although I was feeling a bit uncertain, I reminded myself that God Himself had just spoken to me about marriage. "It must be her," I thought to myself, as I began to reflect upon the many ways in which it made sense that she was the one.

One evening, I finally decided to step out on a limb, call this young woman and ask her out. I was both excited and a tad nervous, but I was sure it would go well. After all, I had a promise.

To my surprise, the response was a definite no. I was flabbergasted. What was going on? What about God's promise?

In the weeks and months to come, I kept trying my very best to connect with this young woman because I was convinced this was God's plan. "Did I approach her the wrong way?" I asked myself. If so, the answer was simple: adopt a different approach. So for the rest of the year, I tried almost every trick in the book. Yet the more I tried, the more firmly I found the door shut, locked and, eventually, completely barred.

I ended the year in despair. "God," I prayed, "I have tried everything in my power to make this happen. Why am I getting nowhere?"

Over time, I began to understand that my very question was hiding the answer. The problem was that I was trying too hard to make God's will come to pass. One painful lesson I learnt from this episode was the danger of entwining God's genuine promises with my own ideas of how they were going to happen. When I took matters into my own hands and my hopes were dashed, I found that my disappointment was intense. So I was learning the hard way that I needed to wait for God to show me His plans before setting my hopes on a particular person.

Sometime later, I found myself coming full circle as a recently divorced woman began to pursue me romantically. She felt strongly that God was telling her that I was the one for her, and she just refused to take my no for an answer, no matter how many times I said it. As she kept pursuing me again and again over a period of time, I came to understand what it is like to be on the receiving end of this kind of pursuit.

It's hard to be in a place where you believe God is speaking to you about a relationship with someone, but that person has not heard the same message and is expressing no interest. My advice to you, in such a situation, is to surrender the matter fully into God's hands and keep your focus on Him. In this way, it will become clear if you may have heard incorrectly about this person in the first place. God also gives people a free will. So even if someone is genuinely called by God to marry you, he or she still has the freedom to say no. Should that person choose to say no, God will still turn this for good in your life and, in His time, will raise up someone else who will be the right match for you.[1]

Being Patient in the Journey

Once my heart had healed from this experience, I was back to waiting for God's promise of marriage. In fact, I wasn't just waiting. I was constantly looking out for who it might be.

I don't know about you, but I've never enjoyed waiting. At times I feel like the preacher who said, "God, give me patience, and give it to me NOW!"

I was about to learn that God truly has a timing for when He acts. But, meanwhile, He was doing exactly what I had asked Him to do - He was preparing me.

In 2005, I enrolled at a local Bible College where one of my assignments was to write a major essay on the subject of my own life. The assignment was to examine each major event in my life, good or bad. I was to evaluate how God had been using it to form me and to build my character for His future purposes.

By the end of my essay, I came to a profound conclusion: God had never done anything in my life without preparing me for it ahead of time. Sometimes I was aware of His preparation and sometimes not. But either way, He was always faithfully and thoroughly preparing me for what He knew was coming up next.

One example was my becoming a youth leader. When I first started my bible studies, it seemed that 'everyone' at College was in youth ministry. That was certainly not something I had ever seen myself doing and I made this very clear to anyone who asked.

One day, our youth leader unexpectedly announced that he was leaving in a few weeks, as he had just received a job offer overseas. When I heard the news, I immediately knew in my heart that God was calling me to fill the vacancy. I asked the Lord to confirm it by having our Pastor approach me about the role and, within days, I was asked to take on the job.

I couldn't have been more surprised to find myself in the role of youth leader. I had never seen myself as youth leader material. Yet, as I started in this new position, I soon discovered that I had a range of skills and experiences that had, in fact, equipped me for the task.

In this example, and in so many other experiences, I found

that God had always prepared me beforehand for His future plan for my life. Even when I felt completely out of my depth, looking back, I could see God's hand lovingly preparing me for what was to come. As a result, I came to the conclusion that God's character means that He never, ever leads us into something without equipping us for the task ahead.

When the Children of Israel left Egypt in the great Exodus, the quickest route they could have chosen to the Promised Land would have led them straight into conflict with the fierce Philistines. The scriptures tell us that God knew that they were not ready to face battle so soon after leaving Egypt (Ex. 13:17). God, therefore, took them on the longer route through the wilderness where He began to prepare them, as a nation, to take possession of the land of Canaan.

This same principle can be seen at work in the lives of many Bible characters, including Joseph, Moses and David. All of these leaders went through unique life experiences which gave them both the skills and the character to handle the challenges that lay ahead.

Through these examples, I began to understand that God was also at work in my life during my waiting season. He was doing a characteristically thorough job in preparing me because He wanted to see me succeed in my future role and be able to withstand the difficulties that would come.

Same Vision and Purpose

One evening, during a time of prayer, I saw a picture of a railway track heading off into the horizon. As I reflected on the picture, I realised that the two parallel metal beams that made up the track were a picture of me and my future wife walking parallel side by side.

The lesson for me was that if my focus were on finding a girl – instead of on pursuing God's purposes – then I could easily find myself moving off track. In addition, if I did go off track to find her, how would I get back on track again?

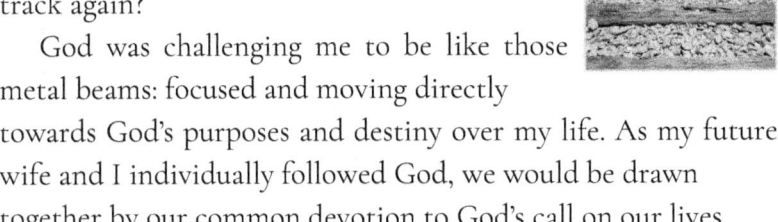

God was challenging me to be like those metal beams: focused and moving directly towards God's purposes and destiny over my life. As my future wife and I individually followed God, we would be drawn together by our common devotion to God's call on our lives.

Vision for Israel

One day, I picked up a book called *The Coming Israel Awakening* by James Goll. The exciting stories and revelations contained in this book began to ignite a passion in me regarding Israel and Bible prophecy. As I pursued this passion and began to learn more, God's call and purpose for my life became a lot clearer. During this time, God gave me a heart for sharing about the Jewish background of our faith and the message that, one day, we can expect Jesus to return. This new and clearer focus for my life may not have shown me whom God intended to be my wife. But it made it a lot easier to know whom God did not have for me because I found that many Christian girls were, quite simply, not on the same track as me.

Six years had now passed since God first gave me the promise of marriage. I felt more ready and prepared than ever. As the seventh year approached, I asked myself, "Is this the year?"

NOTES

[1] For a Biblical example of this, consider the story of King Saul. He was appointed by God to rule as Israel's first king. In fact, the prophet Samuel says that his dynasty on the throne could have lasted forever (1 Sam. 13:13). However, in the end, Saul's ongoing disobedience to God disqualified him from this high calling. And in his place, God raised up David, a man after his own heart.

2

A Chance Encounter

(Enoch writes): Time seemed to have gone by really slowly since God gave me the promise of marriage. I was now in my seventh year of waiting, and it seemed as if I had been waiting forever. "Surely this must be the year?" I thought to myself.

One afternoon, I attended a Jewish historical walk where I took notice of a particular young woman. I assumed that she was a non-Christian like the others on this secular excursion. But when I met her again at a Christian camp later that same week, my curiosity was piqued and I just had to make contact.

As we began to talk, I thought I had struck gold. She was pursuing the same passion as me concerning Israel. Given the spiritual significance of the number seven,[1] I quickly concluded that it must be God bringing her across my path. I mustered my courage and asked her out, and after an initial hesitation, she said yes. I was over the moon!

Over the coming weeks, we went on several dates, and I put all my hopes into this relationship. But despite my wholehearted efforts, we soon found ourselves at loggerheads in heated arguments.

In desperation, I began to pray and as I closed my eyes, I saw a picture of the two of us approaching a T intersection - a dead end where the road forks left and right. My interpretation was that there was no way forward for the two of us. One of us would have to compromise and follow the other person's path or we would be going our separate ways. I knew I couldn't compromise, and soon it became clear that she wouldn't budge either. A few weeks later, we had our last meal together and decided to call it quits.

A Broken Heart Again

I was once again left to pick up the pieces of my broken heart. I was despondent because God's promise of marriage seemed further away than ever. Having started the journey towards marriage with such optimism and hope, I was now feeling so discouraged about the whole thing that I felt like putting my dream on the shelf.

I knew that God had spoken, but I didn't know how to enter into His promise. The more I thought about getting married, the more impossible it seemed, and the worse I felt. I was scared of making more mistakes and running ahead of God. In truth, I was becoming tired of getting my hopes up again and again, only to have them come crashing down to earth with a thud.

The Promise of God - a Weapon of the Enemy

Our adversary, the devil, is a crafty foe, and during this difficult time, he began to use the very promises of God as weapons against me. He would torment me with the thought that it was all my fault. If only I had been better at my interactions with the opposite sex, perhaps God's promise would have come to pass? Maybe I was not handsome enough? Perhaps my financial situation was keeping the right girl at bay? Again and again, the enemy would send his doubts into my mind: doubts concerning the promise; doubts concerning my own ability; and even doubts about ever becoming a husband. In this way, the very promise of God was becoming a potent weapon in Satan's arsenal.

Friends of mine were steadily getting married, and it just seemed so easy for them. I remember looking with envy at a young married couple who were operating beautifully together in a worship ministry. "Why isn't it happening for me?" I asked myself. Here I was with a promise given from God many years ago, and yet I was still single. To make matters worse, I began to imagine that people were looking at me strangely. It felt as if they were whispering things behind my back such as "Why isn't Enoch married yet?" or "Why does he still live at home with his mum?"

Making a depressing situation look even more hopeless was the fact that there were very few eligible women in my circle of friends by now. In fact, I found myself mostly surrounded by women 30 years my senior.

How on earth would I find the right one? And how would I know that my heart would not be broken again?

The Prophetic Blueprint

During this time of soul searching, I wrote a prayer about my future wife on a piece of note paper. Written in November 2011, the prayer simply said:

"*Lord, I ask you for a wife who fears You, has a heart for prayer and worship, has a prophetic calling on her life, has a heart for the nations and is willing to travel and is willing to sacrifice in order to follow You.*"

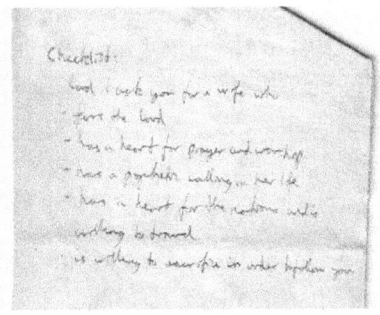

The original bedside prayer

These sentences became my regular prayer week after week, month after month, and year after year during my continued journey of waiting. It was my way of holding onto God's promise and placing before my eyes a divine blueprint of my future wife.

Learning to Know His Leading

Two questions really troubled me during this time. How would I know for sure whom God had for me? And how would I be sure not to make the same, painful mistakes all over again?

A revelation for me came one day as I studied the familiar story of Gideon in the Hebrew Scriptures (the Old Testament). Having been taught from a young age that Gideon's asking for signs was a tale of unbelief not to be followed, I received an "aha" moment as I pondered the fact that Gideon is listed with the heroes of faith in chapter 11 of Hebrews.

Gideon was indeed a champion of faith. The decisions he faced in chapters six and seven of Judges could have imperilled his life, the life of his family and, indeed, the entire nation of Israel. He, therefore, had to be entirely certain of God's leading before stepping out.

How did Gideon arrive at this level of certainty and faith? He did so by asking God for confirmation that it really was God speaking to him and that he was correctly understanding what God wanted him to do.

What was God's response when Gideon asked for confirmation? God didn't knock him on the head and blame him for his unbelief. Instead, God heard his prayer and offered several clear confirmations that Gideon was on the right track. God even exceeded Gideon's requests, ensuring that Gideon knew for sure that this was genuinely God's leading.

Continuing into the New Testament, I saw the same principle again and again. God gladly confirmed His Word with signs following. John explains that the miracles outlined in his Gospel were written so *"that* [we] *might believe"* (John 20:31). As I looked further, I saw that every single time the Bible recorded situations where people asked for confirmation, God graciously provided signs confirming His Word. When John the Baptist expressed doubt over Jesus' ministry, Jesus pointed him to the signs and miracles following His ministry. Even the Pharisees - who were known for their entrenched opposition to Jesus - were given plenty of signs. They saw and witnessed Jesus' many miracles. Yet when they asked, in unbelief, for another sign, Jesus promised them one final sign, the sign of Jonah (i.e., His resurrection.

See Matt. 12:38-42). What greater sign could He possibly have given them?

Understanding that God does confirm His leading to us gave me a confidence that He would, one day, lead me in a similar way of assurance concerning my marriage. First, I could expect God to give me some kind of knowledge about who my future wife was to be. Second, I could expect that He would confirm His Word to me in multiple ways until I knew for sure that it was right. In this way, I could step out like Gideon and trust God to come through and bring me into His destiny for my life.

In line with these principles, I was soon to see God not only bring me and my future wife together, but also make His leading unmistakably clear to me. But before we get to that exciting part of the story, I am going to let Sarah share about her own journey towards the fulfilment of God's promises in her life.

NOTES

[1] The number seven carries great significance in the Bible and is often associated with "the fulfilment of promises and oaths." See *What Is the Biblical Significance of the Number 7?* https://www.christianity.com/wiki/bible/what-is-the-biblical-significance-of-the-number-7.html (accessed Feb 3, 2021).

3

From Heartache to Promise

(Sarah writes): It was 2011 and my brother Matthew and I were about to lose our sole surviving parent.

"If God takes our dad, will you still serve Him?" Matthew asked as he looked at me.

"Yes, I will," I answered confidently.

"And you, Matthew? Will you still serve Him?"

"I will too," Matthew replied.

As we witnessed our beloved father, Tony, draw closer to death, my brother and I were both determined that we would continue to believe in and serve God. We had learnt this lesson from the powerful example set by our father 23 years earlier following our mother's premature death in 1988.

I was born in Carlton, Melbourne. When I was three years

old, my mother, Ngaire, was diagnosed with cancer. At the same time, she had some unexpected and good news. She was pregnant with a baby boy. Facing an agonising choice, mum decided to keep the baby and carry him to full term, but declined chemotherapy for her condition.

Six months after Matthew's birth, my mother's cancer flared up while we were on a family holiday, and she quickly became gravely ill. Although many church friends were praying fervently for us, dad realised that he might soon lose his wife.

One evening as he was out for a walk to clear his head, dad felt God speak to him in his spirit:

"Will you still serve me if Ngaire were to live or die?"

"I don't know," was dad's immediate reply.

He walked a little further and felt God repeat the question,

"Would you still serve me even if Ngaire were to die?"

"I don't want to make a promise if I won't be able to keep it," dad replied.

God spoke to dad a third time: "If I were to give you the grace, the wisdom, the power and the strength, will you still serve Me even if I were to take your wife?"

My dad walked a few more steps and then stopped. He said, "If you give me the grace, the wisdom, the power and the strength, then I will serve you for the rest of my life."

Immediately, my dad felt as if a burden had lifted, and the heavens opened above him, surrounding him with a great light. It was not long after this experience that mum passed away. Dad quickly had to adjust to the new reality of being left on his own to raise us – a four-year old girl and a six-month old boy. Fortunately, our church rallied strongly around our little family, with various mothers volunteering to look after us and cook for us. In fact, for the first few months after mum's death, dad did not have to cook a single meal. Over the next few years, one particular family ended up babysitting little Matthew and me during business hours, which enabled dad to continue his teaching job while knowing we were in good care.

A few years after my mother's death, we moved as a family from Melbourne up north to the Gold Coast. Even though the task of raising my brother and me must have weighed heavily on him, dad was also still mourning the loss of his beloved wife. Dad's way of coping with the grief was to find his comfort and strength in the Lord. After putting us to bed each evening, he would often, in tears, spend hours pouring out his heart before God. He would put on his favourite worship music and found that the touch of God's presence was bringing healing to his broken heart. During this time, dad developed a deep passion for the presence of God.

A New Vision During a Season of Grief

It had now been 23 years since my mother's death, and dad's now deteriorating health was challenging Matthew and me to follow his powerful example of dedication. Would we still serve God if dad passed away? For both of us, the answer was a clear and definite 'yes'.

At 3am on Sunday, 6 November 2011, our precious dad passed on to eternity. Despite the events of the night and only having had a few hours of sleep, I went to church as usual. At the end of a powerful message that Sunday, the pastor opened up the altar for prayer.

I went forward quietly, asking the Lord to give me a new vision and a new dream that I could hang onto in this time of grief. Moments later, as the pastor stood with me, he prayed back to me, word for word. the exact prayer I had just prayed myself.

As the service finished, our youth leader approached me. He was genuinely amazed, asking, "Why of all days are you at church this morning? Most people I know wouldn't even consider turning up to church after what you went through last night."

As I shared with him my decision to follow Jesus, no matter what, I heard the quiet but unmistakeable whisper of the Holy Spirit speaking to my heart. He dropped one Word into my spirit, which was to be the answer to my prayer for a new vision, and the Word was "marriage".

Later that evening, I told a friend about my experience, and she confirmed what I had felt, saying that she had recently seen a vision of my being fitted into a wedding dress.

I had a lot to think about that evening. "Lord, You're not really saying marriage, are you?" I asked.

The next day, an intercessor friend of mine came over for a visit. She said that she had felt the Holy Spirit lead her to bring me a very special gift. I unfurled the wrapping paper and was stunned to see its contents. It was my friend's very own wedding veil from her wedding over 20 years earlier and she was giving it to me to prepare me for my wedding. She had no idea of the vision that God had given me just the day before.

The Honeymoon Package

God truly had unique ways of confirming His Words to me. A few months after receiving the vision for marriage, I went with some girlfriends to a free wedding Expo. As we went from stall to stall, the women at the stalls would ask, "Who is getting married in this group?"

"She's the one," my friends would say, pointing to me.

One stall had a prize competition for brides-to-be. The woman at the stall asked me when I was getting married. I told her that I was hoping to be married sometime in the next 12 months as I entered my name for the competition.

I didn't yet know who my husband would be and felt a bit foolish signing up. But I prayed under my breath, "Lord, if You are saying 'marriage,' let me win."

That afternoon, I got a phone call saying I had won the prize. It was a $1000 honeymoon accommodation package. The conditions of the package were that I had 12 months to book and 18 months to use it (and this was several years before I met Enoch).

Knowing that God was speaking of marriage, I began to wonder if it might be a certain person in my circle of friends. I began to link the time frame for getting married to the time left on the honeymoon package, with high hopes in my heart that it would all happen very soon.

The next few months went slowly by and it eventually became clear that there would be no wedding in time for the honeymoon package. I finally surrendered my expectations concerning this particular man. As I stretched out on my bed that night, I prayed, "Lord, I don't want to marry anyone that You don't have for me." As I quieted myself down, I felt the Holy Spirit speaking to my heart, "It could have been an Ishmael."

This Word told me not only that the person I thought might be my future husband could have been an Ishmael, but also that the time frame I had in mind was wrong. The story of Ishmael in Scripture represents man's way of doing things and here I was trying to tell God what to do and when to do it.

I used the honeymoon package to go on a holiday to Broome with my aunt and brother and later booked a trip to the Cook Islands with the remaining amount. Yet the question remained, "Who was the man that God was going to bring my way and when would it happen?"

Saved from Disaster

During the following years, there were various men who came across my path. Each time, I wrestled with the question whether any of them was the one, but I learnt to stay on my knees, seek godly counsel and follow the Lord's directions in my heart.

If you have been single for years as I was, you will know that sooner or later well-meaning matchmakers will try to get involved. One woman in our church thought she had the solution for me and tried her best to set me up with another member of the congregation. Again, I took the situation to God in prayer, and it slowly became clear that this was not the match that God intended for me either. As I prayed, I understood that not only was I to close the door to him, but I was also to leave this church.

God certainly has a way with timing! To the surprise of everyone, on the very Sunday that I left, this man became the subject of investigation by police for alleged offences. Given the timing of my move, people thought that I must have known something of what was going on, but I had simply followed the Holy Spirit's leading.

Actions of Faith

I believed that God had spoken to me about marriage, and one specific and exciting step of faith I took was to go shopping for a wedding dress. After trying on a few dresses, I finally found the one. It was simple yet elegant and fitted me nicely. The dress turned out to be half the price of all the other dresses I had looked at and I just knew in my heart that this was it.

My friends who were with me were convinced that I was a bit nutty. After all, here I was buying a wedding dress without even having a boyfriend. But faith leads to action, and since I really believed I was getting married, it was only logical for me to get ready the best I could. This included my buying this dress. Little did I know that there would still be another five years before I would get married, and the big question by then would be if I could still fit my dress!

Caleb Company

As I started to prepare for marriage on a practical level, God also began to prepare me spiritually, by clarifying my calling in ministry.

My move to a new church turned out to be very strategic for me when, in 2015, the church hosted a guest speaker called Todd

McDowell from Nashville, USA. He shared about God's love for us as individuals as well as His deep covenantal love for Israel. Todd also shared about his work with a ministry called 'Caleb Company', which takes young people through a one-month training program in the USA followed by a month of ministry and adventure in Israel.

As I heard about this ministry, my heart stirred within me, and I really wanted to take part. Our pastor closed the meeting by announcing that he felt God was calling several of us from our church to be interns on the Caleb Company program. My friends around me were all encouraging me to get involved, but my heart sank and I began to cry as I pondered my circumstances. At that time, I was living as a carer for my then 94-year-old grandfather, and I realised that there was no way I could leave at this stage.

Over the coming months, the desire to go with Caleb Company to Israel just would not go away. One Sunday morning at church, I went forward for prayer and explained my situation. The woman who prayed for me encouraged me to take a practical step forward in faith. So I put in my application, still not knowing how it was going to work out.

Within the month, I was accepted into the program. Meanwhile, due to my grandfather's health, it was decided that he would have nurses coming regularly to assist him. This support meant that I was no longer needed in the same way, and the door was finally open for me to embark on my trip to America and Israel.

I let my boss know about my plans and wasn't sure how he would take the news. Despite being a non-believer, he was excited about the idea and said quite prophetically, "Sarah, I don't see you coming back to this job, but rather continuing to do something with this new thing in your life."

I had set aside part of my inheritance from dad to help pay for my future wedding, but I felt challenged by God to let go of this money and use it to pay for the training program. Although this didn't make sense at the time, it would turn out to be an important investment towards God's call on my life, which in turn would link directly into my future marriage.

Nashville

In 2016, I went to Caleb Company, and the following year I returned to join the program as a leader. The time I spent at Caleb company was fruitful, both on a personal level as well as on a ministry level. Personally, I received much in-depth ministry, which helped heal the trauma of losing my parents. There was one particular teaching session that impacted me greatly. During this session, we were learning how to hear from God and were encouraged to ask the following questions as we read Scripture:

1. What is God revealing of Himself in this text?
2. What is He saying about me?
3. How does this lead me to pray for others?

I followed these simple steps in class as I began to read to myself from Matthew 6:9-13 *"Our Father in heaven."* Those first few words impacted me deeply, and I started weeping. Since the loss of my dad, I had found it hard to relate to God as my Father. As tears were rolling down my face, I received a fresh revelation, deep down in my heart, that God is my living, loving and caring Father.

Jordan and Israel

As part of our summer program in 2017, we were not just going to Israel but also to Jordan. The name Jordan means "lowly place'" and there I had the beginning of a very personal encounter with the Lord. During my devotions in Jordan, I felt the Lord speak to me that He wanted to marry me.

Once we were back in Jerusalem, I decided to spend the next three days fasting and seeking the Lord. At the end of the fast, I went up on the rooftop of our apartment overlooking Jerusalem. It was facing this magnificent prophetic view that I felt His gentle voice repeating the question to my heart, 'Sarah, will you marry Me?' And I said, "Yes, I will!"

After this beautiful and intimate moment with the Lord, I returned downstairs to the rest of my team. They could immediately see a real difference in me, and one of the girls noted how my face had changed. It no longer bore any hardness but instead carried a soft beauty reflecting the peaceful presence of the Lord.

In this encounter, God was teaching me that He calls His sons and daughters, often from downtrodden, lowly places, to become His royal bride. God knew my heart's desire for marriage, but before I could get married, I first had to have this time of re-dedication to Him. This encounter was where I came to know in the depths of my being that, first and foremost, it is all about God. He is my highest love and He is my greatest calling.

What Next?

As I ended my time at Caleb Company, I was returning to Australia with a new vision and mission. During my time at Nashville, I had felt the Holy Spirit say, "Go back to Australia and Israel and start up a Caleb Company of sorts." The phrase "of sorts" was ringing in my ears, and I didn't fully understand what it meant. All I knew was that I was on my way home with a new sense of purpose, which involved connecting young people to God as well as imparting to them His heart for Israel.

What I didn't know then was that the Shalom Israel ministry, which Enoch was by this time heading up in Australia, has a mission statement that is almost identical to that of Caleb Company. As I had found my calling, and Enoch had found his, we were being prepared to walk side by side into the destiny God had for us.

Rebekah and Ten Camels

I have learnt through experience that obedience is the key to being in the right place at the right time.

Back in Australia, a friend told me to contact Rabbi Lawrence Hirsch, who heads up Celebrate Messiah in Melbourne.[1] It turned out that he was looking for a new youth leader, and he asked me if I would consider coming down from the Gold Coast. My friend and I prayed about the offer, and we both felt that I should accept it. That same night, I felt the Lord say that I should not only take the role, but also move to Melbourne in just three weeks' time.

Yet even though I was at peace about my decision, I still found myself getting teary as I considered saying good-bye to my family all over again. But after receiving their go-ahead, I began to pack my belongings. And during the next three weeks, God moved quickly to pave the way for me. My looming credit card debt was fully paid off, and money came in to pay for my flights to Melbourne and for a removalist to transfer my goods down south.

Heading to Melbourne on the plane, I had a feeling that I was like Rebekah in the Bible: the chosen bride coming on the camels from far away to meet her Isaac (see Genesis 24).

Meanwhile in Melbourne

(Enoch writes): I had a feeling around this time that my future wife would be somewhere interstate. "But how will I ever find her?" I wondered to myself.

During these exact three weeks when Sarah was getting ready to come down, I was going through a real challenge in my ministry. I had been a pastor for a few years, but it was becoming clear that I would be unable to keep my pastor title unless I redirected my ministry from Shalom Israel to a local church. In the end, I decided to let go of my ministry title, knowing that it was more important to follow God's call on my life than to have a pastoring credential.

What I didn't know then was that not only was my future

wife on her way to Melbourne, but she had also been given a prophetic Word years earlier that she would be marrying a pastor. Yet God knew. Within these same three weeks, everything turned around for me as I was offered the opportunity to be recognised as a pastor by another denomination. So just as Sarah finished packing her bags to head south, my ministry title was in the process of being fully restored.

It had now been almost seven years since Sarah received her prophetic Word about marriage and almost 14 years since I received mine. All this time, God had truly been at work to prepare us for each other. But now the time had finally come when He was about to bring us together.

NOTES

[1] Celebrate Messiah is a Messianic ministry consisting of Jews who believe in Jesus and who want to share their love of the Messiah, especially with their Jewish brethren. Celebrate Messiah has a congregation in Melbourne, Victoria called Beit HaMashiach (House of the Messiah), which consists of both Jewish and Gentile believers who together worship Yeshua (Jesus) within a Hebrew cultural context and framework.

4

Hope Fulfilled

(Enoch writes): March 2018. It was a Friday night in Melbourne as a small group of believers gathered around a Messianic-style Shabbat meal.[1] I had been invited to be the guest speaker for the evening and took my seat at the head of the U-shaped table. The evening began with the lighting of the Sabbath candles, followed soon after by traditional prayers of blessing and songs of praise welcoming the peace of God into the room. And so it was, in a setting which speaks of ceasing from our own striving and entering into God's finished work, that I finally met Sarah.

From the start of the event, I had noticed her. I had never seen her before, but there was something about Sarah that caught my eye and kept my attention. At the end of the event, it became clear that she needed a lift home and my Mum promptly offered our assistance.

On the way, Sarah began to share the express version of

her life story, and I was stunned by what I heard. During our 30-minute car ride, I discovered that she had the very traits I had been praying for all these years in my future wife. I felt quite literally as if I were standing on holy ground, and I knew, in my heart, that God was about to do something.

Soon Sarah and I began to communicate a lot via email and then text messages. It felt crazy pursuing Sarah. After all, I really knew nothing about this girl who had come down from the Gold Coast only a few months before we met. However, the more I got to know her, the more I could see confirmation after confirmation that God was bringing us together. "Was God speaking to her about me as well?" I wondered to myself, as our contact began to flourish.

Sarah's Dance

(Sarah writes): By the time I met Enoch, I was well and truly sick of my never-ending questions about which man would be the right one. My prayer was that when I met the right one, I would have a week of not constantly asking myself the question, "Is it him?"

After I met Enoch, my prayer came true. I actually had a whole week of not wondering about it at all and then, at the end of the week, as I spent some time in worship, I felt Enoch's name come clearly to mind.

As I continued to worship, I began to dance, imagining that I was dancing with Jesus. During the dance, I felt Him say in my heart, "Enoch. I will hand you over to him."

This experience of worship dancing with Jesus brought me

back to a similar time of dancing five years earlier. During that previous experience, I felt the Holy Spirit clearly say, "I will hand you over to him" (meaning my future husband).

Faith Like Hannah

One night, roughly two weeks after meeting Enoch, I was lying on my bed trying to sleep, but my mind was wide awake. "When did I get that Word about being a Hannah?" I thought to myself.

This took me back to my time as part of a ministry team in Nashville, USA the previous year (2017). At that time, and after a long and difficult journey, a close friend of mine had just seen God move on her behalf to bring her together with the one who would later become her husband. When she told me the happy news, I found myself breaking down in tears. Over the next few days, I just couldn't help crying whenever I saw these two lovebirds happily together. I was honestly trying my best to be happy for her, yet at the same time my heart was deeply longing for the fulfilment of my own promise.

One of our Nashville ministry team members spoke prophetically right into my life saying, "Sarah, I see you as a Hannah. I see you as someone who has deep faith. There have been Elis in your life who have mocked or questioned your faith. But God wants you to know that He sees your faith, that it is real and it is very deep." Just as Hannah in the Bible had wept in anguish for God's promise in her life, so I too had come to the point of tears while waiting for God to move.

Two days later, I felt the Holy Spirit speak to me in a similar vein: "I see your longing, I hear and I know." The next morning, I went to church, and the pastor gave a message from Proverbs 13:12 that spoke straight to my heart about hope fulfilled. He pointed out that although some of us had been through a journey of hope deferred, the full verse says: "*Hope deferred makes the heart sick, but a longing fulfilled is a tree of life.*"(NIV). In other words, there is coming a day when God's promises will come to pass in our lives and that will be like a breath of fresh air for us.

At the end of his message, the pastor said, "I hear the Holy Spirit say: 'I hear, I see, I have not forgotten.'" In that moment, I knew that this blessing and this message were for me.

Just as Eli, the priest, blessed Hannah and promised that she would have her request, so I felt that this pastor, through the Holy Spirit, was speaking God's blessing over me. And from that day on, I personally found that like Hannah of the Bible, my countenance had changed.[2] I now had a knowing assurance that God had heard and that He would answer.

God's Timing

With all these thoughts about my resemblance to Hannah running through my mind, I was still lying in bed trying to sleep. But my curiosity got the better of me and I pulled out my calendar. I was given the Hannah prophecy in June 2017.

Counting back from the present date in March 2018 made it nine months earlier. I thought to myself, "Wait a second. When exactly in June?"

I worked out that it was 9 June 2017. The day I met Enoch in Melbourne at the Sabbath meal was 9 March 2018. So just as Hannah gave birth to Samuel nine months after God heard and remembered her heart-felt prayers, so too God had me meet Enoch nine months to the day after speaking His reassuring Word to me.

Seven Years to the Month

(*Enoch writes*): By now, I was feeling certain that Sarah was the one and was beginning to think of buying an engagement ring. But how would I find out her ring size without spoiling the surprise? Well, luckily for me, not long after, Sarah began to show me some rings she had bought in Israel. I casually and coolly examined the rings while secretly making note of her ring size. A few days later, I put in the order for a beautiful engagement ring.

As I waited for the ring to be prepared, I began to pray about a potential date for our wedding. I don't normally get dates and figures when I pray. But this time, I felt I got a very clear date – 11 November 2018.

Pondering the significance of this date, I asked myself a rather curious question. "When was it that I wrote my prayer about my future wife?" This was the prayer that I had been praying again and again all these years. I rummaged through my records and discovered, to my surprise, that I had written the prayer in November 2011. Interesting. That would make it seven years exactly to the month for us to get married.

All of this was, of course, still 'top secret information,' and there was no way I was going to say anything yet to Sarah about my discovery. But a few days later, Sarah and I met up for a coffee. Unexpectedly and without cue, she began to share with me about the significance of November 2011 in her life. I was all ears as she told me about her dad's passing away at that time and how she received the vision for marriage in that very month.

Needless to say, I was floored. In that moment, I realised that at the very time that I wrote down my prayer in Melbourne for a future wife, God had begun to speak to Sarah on the Gold Coast. And here she was seven years later as the answer to my prayers. How true it is that from the very moment we pray, God hears and is at work, answering our prayers.

During all this time, when I was often tempted to lose hope, God had been faithfully at work to bring about the fulfilment of His promise in my life. There and then, I said a quick prayer in my heart, repenting for all the times I had doubted God during this journey.

Sitting in the coffee shop with Sarah that day, I could hardly contain my excitement. "If only I had the ring in my pocket," I thought, "I would be proposing right now!"

The Poet Awakens

Over the next few weeks, while I was still waiting for the ring to arrive, God began to show me that He is also a God of romance. Having shown me beyond doubt that Sarah was my wife to be, He was now teaching me how to win her heart. Words began to form in my mind, and before I knew it, I had written my very first poem, a love poem to Sarah.

"Sarah, Sarah, who is fairer?" was the title of the poem. As I read her the poem, Sarah was very touched and felt in her heart that God was using this special moment to confirm that He was about to hand her over to me.

A Special Horse and Carriage Ride

Finally, the ring arrived, and a few days later, I took Sarah into the city where a horse and carriage ride was waiting for us. I had chosen this day as it would have been Sarah's mother's 62nd birthday. In the carriage, I told Sarah that I was sorry that I would never get to meet her mum. "The best I can do in honour of her," I explained as I got down on one knee, "is to promise to look after you all the days of my life." I brought out the ring and popped the big question: "Sarah, will you marry me?"

"YEEESSSS!!!" was the definite answer that resounded in the carriage as Sarah and I warmly embraced.

We had decided to refrain from kissing until we got married. And so it was that six months later, as the minister said, 'You may now kiss the bride', Sarah and I shared our first kiss to seal our union.

NOTES

[1] The Hebrew word for 'Sabbath' is 'Shabbat'. Shabbat is celebrated from Friday at sundown until Saturday at sundown. Jewish Shabbat gatherings typically feature ancient Jewish traditions and practices for honouring this special day, many of which date back to the days of Yeshua (or Jesus). Messianic Shabbat gatherings keep many of these same traditions, but interpret them in light of Yeshua's teachings while adding in modern worship practices.

[2] For more of Hannah's story, see 1 Sam. 1:1-18.

5

Are you Waiting for a Promise to be Fulfilled?

(*Enoch writes*): Many of you who are reading this book will be at different stages on your own journey towards the fulfilment of your own promise. In this section, I would like to address those various stages and give advice based on the lessons that Sarah and I have learnt. I have grouped the suggestions below based on four possible scenarios.

I Have a Dream

Do you have a deep and unfulfilled desire in your life? Perhaps it is about getting married, having a baby or being involved in a particular field of ministry?

The first and most difficult question you will have to ask

yourself about such a desire is whether it really is in God's specific blueprint for your life. The fact that you have a desire for something doesn't automatically mean that this is exactly what God has in mind for you. It is very hard to distinguish between our own desires and what God is saying. The first step, therefore, is truly to let go of and surrender your dream to God. I'm not saying that laying it down will be easy. But I know that it is only as your expectations are put to the side that you will be in a place to hear more clearly what God wants to say.

You may not be used to hearing from God personally. Yet I believe that He wants to make His direction and guidance clear to all of us as His children. It takes time to learn to hear from God. We develop the ability to discern His voice as we spend time with Him in His Word, hear teaching from anointed ministries and learn to obey Him in small matters.

As I explained earlier in this book, when it comes to the big questions of life (such as whom to marry), God can and will confirm His Word and His promise to you. Ask Him for these confirmations and let Him confirm His Word to you in His way and His time.

I Already Have a Specific Promise From God

If you believe you have a clear Word from God and have received confirmations of this Word, then you can trust that God is already at work to bring this promise to fulfilment. You may find that your journey of waiting for the promise to be met is relatively short and easy. Or it may involve a longer and more challenging route such as the one that Sarah and I experienced.

Either way, you can be sure that God will use this waiting time to prepare you to receive the fulfilment of the promise.

But while you are waiting, I would warn you to be careful not to mix God's genuine promise with your own expectations as to how or when that promise might be fulfilled. From my own experience, I know how challenging it can be to unscramble such a mixture of divine promise and personal wishes and come back to a point of real clarity as to what God is actually saying.

I've Been Waiting Many Years

Years may have passed since you received your divine promise, yet seeing its fulfilment may seem more distant than ever. If you are in this situation, I would like to encourage you that God is indeed a faithful, promise-keeping God and that the fulfilment will come in His perfect timing.

If you haven't done so already, I would suggest that you write down your promise on a piece of paper and make it a habit to thank God regularly that He is working towards its fulfilment. Taking these simple steps will help counteract any doubts that the enemy may want to place in your mind. Take time also to thank God for your present circumstances and to acknowledge that He is turning the situation around for good (see Rom. 8:28).

Remember also to keep pursuing God and His purpose for your life as you wait. Some people pledge to serve God wholeheartedly only once they receive their heart's desire. But God is looking for those who will faithfully serve Him even while longing for the fulfilment of the promise in their lives. Serving Him with all your heart in this season will build character and faithfulness in your life whilst also positioning you to be in the right place to receive the fulfilment of God's plan.

I've Had Doubts and Made Mistakes

Welcome to the club! Listening to some testimonies of people who have experienced God's miracles in their lives, you may think that they have never had their moments of doubt and unbelief. In sharing our story as honestly as possible, I have tried to make it clear that we certainly were not one of them. Like many of you, we had our doubts, and we made our mistakes even after receiving an unmistakeable promise from the Almighty.

Do doubts and mistakes disqualify us from seeing the promise come to pass? The Scriptures show us that this is not the case. Israel, the chosen nation of God, has a history littered with mistakes, doubts and unfaithfulness to God. Yet, in writing about his own people, even after many of them had rejected Jesus as the Messiah, the Apostle Paul explains that, *"the gifts and callings of God are irrevocable"* (Rom. 11:29). In other words, Israel's mistakes did not disqualify them from God's call on their lives. Nor do your doubts and mistakes disqualify you once you confess and repent of them. Despite Israel's failures, God is still at work to bring about His promises to them, and He will do the same for you and me.

In the same way, we can take comfort from Abraham's story. Abraham made a serious mistake with Hagar, which was spurred on by his own doubts about God's promise that his elderly wife, Sarah, would bear him a son. Yet, despite Abraham's obvious flaws and weaknesses, God not only brought about the fulfilment of His promise, but also made Abraham a strong example of faith to all of us. So, if you have been struggling to believe, or you have made mistakes along the way, shift your focus back to God. Yes, you may not have been perfect. But God remains faithful, and He is still able to bring about His promise to you in His time and His way. In the process, He will build faith in your life so that you, too, can one day be an inspiration to others.

I'm Feeling Discontented

1 Timothy 6:6 says: "*Godliness with contentment is great gain.*" The message here is that God doesn't just want us to live godly lives. He also wants us to live contented lives. But this is where the enemy has set a clever trap for many who are waiting for a promise to be met. His trap is to make us long so much for the fulfilment of the promise that we are discontented with the present. I wasted much time carrying this attitude until one day God highlighted this verse to me, and I repented of my discontentment. I committed myself, for the remainder of my waiting period, to be happy in the present while looking, with joyful expectation, to the future He had for me.

From then on, I began to pray the following prayer on a regular basis:

"God, I thank you for your plans for me and for my future wife. I look forward to getting married as you have promised. But I also thank you that right now I am single. I thank you for the good plans You have for me and pray that You will use me today for Your glory."

If you are waiting for marriage, this prayer may also be helpful for you. But it can be adapted to any promise which God has made to you or even to cases where you are still seeking a Word from God.

A Final Word of Advice

No matter where you are at on your journey, I would like to encourage you to remember that, from God's perspective, the journey is as important as the destination. As you go through this period of waiting, try to remember that God doesn't just want to fulfil His promise to you. True to His nature, He is taking you on an important journey of preparation, which will equip you to inherit and enjoy the full manifestation of His promises.

Looking back, Sarah and I truly thank God that we didn't come together any earlier than we did, because we both needed the time to learn some important lessons first. As we will share in the next chapter, we encountered some very tough challenges not long after we got married. As a result, we now see the wisdom in waiting as long as we did.

6

A Fairy Tale Ending

(*Enoch writes*): The handsome prince meets the lovely princess, they get married in a fairy tale wedding and live happily ever after...

Are fairy tales for real? Our honeymoon in New Zealand certainly felt like it. I had never been to New Zealand before, and on arriving in Queenstown, I was awestruck by the beauty of this tiny country. Driving our hire car along spectacular, scenic roads on our way to our honeymoon destination, I had tears in my eyes as I contemplated God's goodness in my life. After so many years of waiting, I was finally married to my beautiful wife, and now I found myself on a honeymoon in stunning New Zealand. Wow!

Although our honeymoon felt like such a fitting end to our long journey of waiting, I also knew that it was only the beginning of a new chapter in our lives. As it happens, marrying Sarah did not mean that there would be no more problems in my life or hers. I was soon to learn that the Promised Land God had for us – like the land He gave to Israel – contained giant-size challenges greater than either of us had ever experienced before.

Are there Twins in the Family?

A few months after our wedding, Sarah discovered that she was pregnant. At the time, an intercessor friend, who knew nothing yet of our news, told my mum that she felt it was time for Sarah and me to have a baby. Then she went on to ask a very curious question: "Are there twins in the family?"

Six weeks later, Sarah was at the doctor's for a check-up, and she mentioned this story. The doctor promptly pulled out an ultrasound machine, saying, "Let's find out!" Within moments, the ultrasound showed first one tiny baby and then another one developing inside Sarah.

Sarah and I were overjoyed at the news, but the next few months were very challenging for Sarah as she struggled with severe morning sickness, hypo-thyroidism and depleted energy levels. It was an important time for me to stand with Sarah, to pray for her, minister to her and offer practical and loving support.

Sarah's pregnancy certainly was a long and hard journey for us. But nothing could take away our joy as we celebrated the arrival of our twins on 10 November 2019, the day before our first wedding anniversary. We named our gorgeous duo David and Hannah.

Sarah's dad had been a twin and now God was bringing a fresh set of twins into his family line. To us, it was clear that God was redeeming what had been lost. He was turning the sorrow over the death of Sarah's father into a time of joyful celebration of God's goodness in our lives. From now on, the month of November would always mark the fulfilment of God's promises to us of marriage. It would also be the month in which we would celebrate the addition to our family of our two precious babies.

Enoch and Sarah with Hannah and David

Stretched to the Limit

Caring for one baby is hard work, but we soon discovered that caring for two can push you to your limit. It can take up to an hour and a half to feed and re-settle one new born baby;

then an hour and a half for the other baby; and then it is time to feed the first baby again. We soon found ourselves in constant demand day and night, changing nappies, doing feeds and trying to catch up on some sleep in the short breaks we were given.

We were also under increasing financial pressure because my level of income was no longer enough to provide for our growing needs. On top of it all, Sarah and I were trying to find our way as newly-weds and still had adjustments to make in our relationship with each other.

It certainly was not easy, and it did not take long before we both began to slide downhill emotionally. One morning, as we cried out to God in desperation for help, a woman spontaneously offered to come and help us at nights. We had not dared to dream that anyone would do that for us and were in tears as we accepted her offer. Soon she started spending six nights a week with us as a volunteer, which made a huge difference. We also received help from family and friends. Yet, despite all this, we still found ourselves frequently stretched to breaking point with the mounting pressures we were facing.

Giants in the Promised Land

When the people of Israel first heard of the giants in the land of Canaan, they were so terrified that they wanted to return to Egypt.[1] Similarly, we had our own tearful moments when we wished ourselves out of the intense challenges we were now facing, day in and day out. Yet this was the Promised Land God had for us. And these were the challenges God had been preparing us to face during our journey towards marriage. Knowing that God had led us together and knowing that this was His plan for us, we therefore trusted that He would somehow help us through to the other side.

During this time, I found that God had equipped Sarah to be just the right person to stand with me when I was feeling overwhelmed. Similarly, she found that I was able to understand and pray with her with a maturity that she had not experienced in other men of my age. God had truly known what He did when He brought us together. In the end, we were able to emerge out of this challenging season with a new strength in the Lord and in each other.

Let God Prepare You

Although Hollywood presents a glamorous picture of life after we meet the woman or man of our dreams, nothing could be further from the truth. Married life is not easy. Add to that the challenge of parenting, should that occur, and you may find that you are in one of the most testing seasons of your life. We would, therefore, encourage those of you who are currently single not to rush into marriage, nor to be impatient as you wait for your future life partner.

Looking back, Sarah and I are grateful for the time of waiting that we experienced. We both had our moments of impatience and frustration. But through the journey, we got to know God better, discovered our purpose in Him, and learnt to trust His voice and His promise, even when nothing made sense. All this prepared us for the day when we would finally meet. And it enabled us to step by faith into the marriage that God had for us.

So our message to those of you who are waiting is to take heart and take courage. God has truly heard your prayer and the answer is on the way. Don't despise the journey you are on or the waiting period you are going through, because, in truth, God is preparing you right now for His promises.

Allow God to continue to prepare you in this waiting season because the journey ahead, after you say "I do", is going to be more challenging than you can imagine. Despite this, when you know that God has led you on this path, it can also become the most fruitful season of your life.

We wish you well on the journey ahead!

NOTES

[1] See Num. 13:1-2, 31-33, 14:1-4.

7

The Big Picture: Messiah and His Bride

> *"Marriage is the beautiful design of the Almighty, a great and sacred mystery - meant to be a vivid example of Christ and his church"* (Eph. 5:32, Passion Translation).

While marriage is beautiful in and of itself, God has also designed it to demonstrate key aspects of His own nature.

"For better or for worse, in sickness and in health, til death do us part," or similar phrases, are part of wedding vows exchanged by couples all over the world. This kind of covenantal love mirrors God's undying love to us as His people.[1] He is truly with us for better or for worse. He is with us in sickness and in health. And He will be with us even as we step from earth into eternity.

Marriage also provides a safe environment in which to raise children, one in which both parents model God's love to their precious offspring. Although the role of a mother cannot be underestimated, fathers leave indelible images of the nature of God the Father in their children's minds. Children who have grown up disappointed and angry with their fathers often struggle to comprehend God as a loving Father. This is why being a father is such an important role.[2]

Marriage is not only intended to provide a setting in which to demonstrate God's love to His creation, including children. It is also meant to be a living, breathing picture of the love of the Messiah for His bride, the Church. Paul explains in chapter five of Ephesians that husbands are to nourish and cherish their wives (verse 29) and to love them self-sacrificially, just as the Messiah loves His Church (verse 25). Modelling the example of Jesus' love towards our wives is a high calling for us men. While this commandment might seem lofty and even impossible in practice, God's intention is that we should depend on Him for its achievement. In this way, it will truly be His love that shines through us to our wives.

Ancient Jewish Wedding Customs

There is more to this picture of the Messiah and His bride that is only revealed if we examine the Jewish cultural background in the time of Jesus.[3]

The Betrothal

Back then, the arrangement of a Jewish marriage would all

begin with a young man's parents searching out a potential bride for their son. When he found a possible match, his father would respectfully approach her father and negotiate a bridal price. In true Middle Eastern style, they would bargain back and forth over the price.

"One camel, two chickens and a milk cow," the father of the young man might offer.

"I'm sure you can do better than that," the other father would perhaps say. "After all, we have looked after her for 16 years and she is very beautiful."

"Ok, I will add in four more chickens and a goat."

"It's a deal," the father of the bride might reply.

Once the price had been set, a time would be arranged for the young man to meet his intended. He would bring with him a written copy of the proposed marriage covenant, also known in Hebrew as a 'ketubah'. In this document, he would spell out his obligations should she consent to the marriage. She would then be presented with a cup of wine, and if she chose to accept and drink of the cup, they would be formally engaged.

Engagement in those times meant a lot more than it does nowadays. It meant that they were practically as good as married, yet not living together until the marriage ceremony took place.

In His last meal with His disciples, Jesus presented them with a cup. This cup would have carried many meanings to them, but one of the most profound would have been drawn from this engagement ceremony. In particular, drinking from this cup would have meant saying "yes" to Jesus' covenant - His ketubah - and "yes" to being engaged to Him.

Preparation for the Wedding

Once the intended bride had signalled her acceptance by taking the cup, the young man would depart back to his father's house. There he would build a room annexed to the house. The bride would be left to wait in anticipation. Yet the custom was that she would not know the time of his return.

The groom would, understandably, be excited about fetching his bride, but first he would have to get approval from his father that the room he had prepared was ready. Every so often, the excited (and increasingly impatient) young man might ask his father to inspect the room.

"Abba,[4] come and look at the room now! I've fixed up the walls and I've added a sturdy roof. Can I go and get my bride?"

"Hmmm," the father might say as he carefully inspected the room: "Son, you have to work more on this wall. Look at the crack that is already forming."

As a result, months might go by as the son would work hard on preparing the room for his chosen bride. Meanwhile, the young woman would not be sitting idle either, but would be busy preparing her wedding garments for her big day. She knew that her handsome groom could arrive at any time, and she also knew that it was customary for the young man to arrive, without notice, in the middle of the night. So like many other young brides, she might sleep in her complete wedding outfit so she would be ready, at a moment's notice, to come out and meet the bridegroom.

Back at the father's house, and after finally receiving the tick of approval for the bridal chamber, the young man would gather a group of his friends and travel to fetch his bride. Announcing the groom's surprise arrival into town late at night, his friends would sound blasts of the shofar (ram's horn). After arriving at the house of his bride, the excited groom would take his ready and prepared bride back to his father's house where an extravagant, seven-day wedding feast would await.

Jesus drew heavily on these wedding traditions when He explained to His disciples that He was going to leave them to go to His Father and that He was going *to prepare a place* for them (John 14:2-3). They were told to expect that, just like a bridegroom, He would one day suddenly return, at a time known only by His Father (Matt. 24:36), to take them to be with Him. Jesus' message to them, as well as to us today, is that we need to be like a wise bride, who is found ready and waiting when that great day arrives (see, for example, Matt. 24:37-44, 25:1-13).

A Modern Example

We have seen how the prophetic symbolism of Jesus' departure from earth and His return for His bride beautifully entwine with ancient Jewish marriage practices. Marriage is truly intended to be a picture of a far greater reality: the love of the Messiah for His Bride – us, His beloved. In this way, each marriage, each love story, and even, I believe, the longing to find a mate is intended by God to point us to a far greater love story.

To further understand this symbolism, we can turn to the modern day story of Brayden and Tali Waller, who chose to go through a uniquely prophetic journey to marriage. They decided to make a film of their experience in order to share their beliefs and insights with others.[5] This young couple - with the blessing of their parents - hosted a beautiful and emotional betrothal ceremony attended by family and friends. After the couple pledged their love to each other, washed each other's feet, publicly read their marriage ketubah (covenant) and shared in communion, the ceremony ended on a sad note as Brayden solemnly rose to his feet to announce that he was leaving. The camera followed Tali's face as Brayden left the room and, from that point onwards, the young couple had no direct face-to-face contact until the time of their marriage ceremony. Being a builder, Brayden quite literally went to work on preparing their future house during this waiting period.

As the months went by, it was increasingly evident how much Tali was yearning and longing to be with her future husband. Finally, the house was completed, and arrangements were made for the families, on both sides, to spend a week at a camping ground. In keeping with the ancient Jewish tradition, the groom would appear at an unspecified time during the week and the bride would have to make sure she was ready. The excitement and longing was increasingly intense during this week until, finally, everyone heard the sounding of the shofar (trumpet) echoing through the camp ground. Tali led the way as her friends and family members gathered at the appointed meeting place, waiting in anticipation for what was about to happen next. Gasps and applause arose from the crowd as they spotted the groom in the distance, riding on a stunning white horse and flanked by his groomsmen, carrying their shofars.

On arriving at the gathering, Brayden descended from his horse and embraced his beloved Tali. As they finally met again, they quite simply couldn't stop smiling and gazing at each other.

Finally, the journey was complete, the separation was over, and they would now spend the rest of their lives together.

The Waiting Period

The betrothal and marriage ceremony are metaphors for Jesus' return. You and I, like Tali, are waiting for our future bridegroom. But we are waiting for the most glorious bridegroom of all history, Jesus. He is the One who loves us with the greatest love ever possible.

Being recently married myself, I know that at a wedding, it is not just the bride who is excited. The groom can also hardly wait to see, and be with, his beloved bride. Jesus has been waiting all this time for His Father to give Him the go-ahead to come and fetch His beloved bride – you and all those who have acknowledged Him to be the Messiah. He loves you intensely and passionately and is more excited over you than you can ever imagine. He can't wait to see you, clothed in white and in splendour, and to be with you.

Yet despite this, some Christians still do not see themselves as Jesus sees them. They walk through life with their heads bowed in shame. They feel condemned over their past, they feel inferior, and some even feel like failures. Although they acknowledge and praise Jesus, their view of themselves is very low. Dear believer, you need to know and understand that your sins – once confessed – have been truly washed away. From Heaven's perspective, you are truly clothed in sparkling white garments. You are part of the glorious bride, and your heavenly bridegroom can't wait to see you.

So let us learn to live like Tali: excited, ready, and waiting, with eager anticipation, for that special day which is coming. Let us set ourselves apart for God only, being ready day or night for His arrival!

The Hope of His Return

Jesus has promised to return for His bride at a time known only to the Father (Matt. 24:36). Some churches and traditions have simply never placed any emphasis on this topic. But, unfortunately, other bible teachers down through the ages have set their own dates as to when Jesus would come. In expectation, people have sold houses and left jobs, only to experience profound disappointment as the chosen date has passed with no sign of Jesus' return. In disillusionment, therefore, many churches have avoided the topic of Jesus' return altogether and have focused their teaching instead on the here and now.

Either way, this lack of sound teaching leaves many believers unprepared for the fulfilment of the promise of Jesus' return. But the promise of His return is not intended to be merely a theological statement of belief. It is meant to propel us right now to the lifestyle of an expectant bride.

My wife Sarah's hope of marriage caused her to buy a wedding dress five years ahead of time. What would we change in our lives if we really believed that Jesus was coming again in the near future? John, the Apostle, writes that the hope of His coming *"purifies us"* (1 John 3:3). How does it purify us? It causes us to live differently; it causes us to live prepared. When we sin, the expectation of His return causes us to repent quickly and challenges us to change our behaviour. And as we live life this way, we are, from Heaven's perspective, ready and waiting, clothed spiritually-speaking in splendid white garments of holiness and righteousness.

Signs Confirming

At the end of Chapter two, I used several scriptural examples to show how God gives confirmations to assure us of the veracity of His Word. I explained that God doesn't want to leave us in the dark, trying to guess what He wants us to do. Rather, He gladly confirms His leading. This principle also applies to Jesus' return.

Not only has Jesus repeatedly told us in the Bible that He is coming, but He has also given us clear signs to watch for to indicate that we are getting closer to that day. It is, therefore, our duty, as an expectant bride, to stay alert for these signs and prepare our lives accordingly.

There are many signs to watch for, including: the rise of deception; false prophets and false Messiahs (Matt. 24:4-5, 11); the increasing persecution of believers (Matt. 24:9); and a great falling away from the faith (2 Thes. 2:3). Many of these signs are already happening before our eyes. For example, a woman in China is claiming to be the returned Jesus, and millions are following her aggressive cult known as Eastern Lightning.[6] Similarly, in Russia, a man calling himself 'Vissarion' is claiming to be Jesus and has gathered a large following in Siberia.[7] Persecution of believers is heating up across much of the Islamic world while liberal, western democracies are also becoming increasingly intolerant towards those of us who hold Biblical values. Regarding the great 'falling away,' the advent of Darwinism and the teaching of evolution have been responsible for a massive decline in faith across the western world, leading us to what is now commonly called a 'post-Christian civilization'.[8]

On a more positive note, another sign that we are getting closer to Jesus' return is the preaching of the gospel to all nations or ethnic groups (Matt. 24:14). Right now, missionaries and bible translators are using the latest technologies to share the message of Jesus to the remaining unreached people groups on this planet. It is only a matter of time before the gospel has reached all ethnic groups.

The Sign of Israel

I personally believe that one of the clearest and most important signs we can watch for is what is happening in the nation of Israel. Jesus promised to return to Jerusalem, not to Brussels, New York or Sydney. However, He set a condition on His return, saying to His Jewish disciples at that time: *"You shall see Me no more till you say, 'Blessed is He who comes in the name of the Lord!'"* (Matt 23:39). In other words, Jesus' return is contingent on all of Israel welcoming Him back.

For this to happen, the Jews first had to return to Israel from their long exile in the nations (all other non-Jewish countries outside Israel). No other people in history have ever come back to their land after suffering such a long exile and after enduring so much persecution down through the ages. Yet many Scriptures foretold that the Jewish people would one day return from the nations (Deut. 30:4, Isa. 11:11-12, Jer. 31:8-10). And true to God's Word, the majority of the world's Jews are now back in the land of their forefathers.[9]

Having returned to Israel, Jews are, for the first time since the days of the Apostles, turning to their Messiah in significant numbers. In recent times, evangelistic videos featuring believing Jews sharing their stories of faith have been produced in Hebrew and gone viral on the internet. Although Israel has a population of only six million Hebrew speakers, these videos have been watched over 6.4 million times in 2020 alone.[10] Israel is also facing constant pressure from hostile nations around her and from the global community. All this is bringing the people of Israel closer to a situation where they will be ready to welcome back their Messiah as Scripture has foretold.

Getting Ready

We have seen how marriage is designed by God and how the ancient Jewish wedding customs beautifully foreshadow Jesus' promised return for us, His bride. We have also examined Biblical signs of Jesus' impending return and have seen that many of these signs are already happening right before our eyes. It is, therefore, more important than ever that we live prepared for Jesus' return.

What should we do then? Like a bride, let us keep our love for our heavenly bridegroom centre-stage in our lives. We can do this by spending time in the Word every day and fellowshipping with Him in prayer.

We can also keep ourselves ready for Him by ensuring that our relationships are in order with the people around us, including our families and friends, work colleagues and fellow believers. To do this, we need to be quick to deal with any offense or unforgiveness. Similarly, it is important to deal with any other sin issues in our lives. If you are really struggling with overcoming damaging or hurtful habits or addictions, it is time to seek help and have other mature believers or leaders stand with you in prayer so you can walk in freedom. Getting help is a big step; but be assured that as you genuinely repent, God will forgive your sins and help you to turn away from wrongful patterns of behaviour.

Communion

Another very practical way to live a life ready for Jesus' return is by taking communion regularly. You can do this on your own in your home or with others in a small group or at church. Communion is always a great opportunity to examine our hearts and ensure we are in right relationship with God and with the people around us.

In addition, as you take communion, I would encourage you to reflect on the story of the ancient Jewish wedding. As you recall the custom of a young woman saying yes to a wedding proposal by accepting the cup, picture yourself saying 'yes' to Jesus as you take the cup of communion. As His bride, recommit yourself to waiting expectantly for Him, and receive Him afresh as your Heavenly bridegroom. As you finish communion, picture yourself clothed in a beautiful white wedding garments. This symbolises that you have been cleansed from the sin of your past and are now living ready for His return.

One day, you and I will truly stand face to face with our glorious Bridegroom. May we be found ready and waiting when that day comes.

NOTES

[1] For more on Covenants and Marriage, see *Marriage Covenant: The Biblical Secret for a Love That Lasts* by Derek Prince.

[2] For more on Fatherhood, see *Husbands & Fathers: Rediscover the Creator's Purpose for Men* by Derek Prince.

[3] If you would like more insight into these ancient customs, especially as they relate to the Galileans of Jesus' day, see *The Best Day of Forever: Jesus, A Galilean Wedding And The End Of The World* by Jay McCarl.

[4] Abba is Hebrew for 'father' or 'daddy'. See *What Does 'Abba' Really Mean?* https://blog.logos.com/what-does-abba-really-mean/ (accessed Feb 5, 2021).

[5] Their story is available on the DVD *Betrothed* available from https://www.loveandpurity.com/product-page/betrothed-movie-dvd.

[6] *Eastern Lightning*, https://en.wikipedia.org/wiki/Eastern_Lightning (accessed Jan 22, 2021).

[7] *Vissarion*, https://en.wikipedia.org/wiki/Vissarion (accessed Jan 22, 2021).

[8] Much has been written on the impact of Darwinism. A good starting point is J. Marinus' article *The Effects of Darwinism on Church and Society*. https://www.christianstudylibrary.org/article/effect-darwinism-church-and-society (accessed Jan 29, 2021).

[9] For more on this, I recommend the book *The Coming Israel Awakening* by James Goll.

[10] *A Record-Breaking Breakthrough Year In Israel*, Nov 25, 2020 https://www.oneforisrael.org/israel/a-record-breaking-breakthrough-year/ (accessed Jan 22, 2021).

Selected Bibliography

Recommended Books on Marriage

Eggerichs, Emerson. *The Language of Love & Respect: Cracking the Communication Code with Your Mate.* Grand Rapids, MI: Thomas Nelson Publishers, 2009.

Ludy, Eric. *The First 90 Days of Marriage.* Denver, CO: W Publishing Group, 2006.

Omartian, Stormie. *The Power of a Praying Wife.* Nashville, TN: Harvest House Publishers, 2017.

Prince, Derek. *God Is a Matchmaker: Seven Biblical Principles for Finding Your Mate.* Ada, MI: Chosen Books, 2011.

Prince, Derek. *Husbands & Fathers: Rediscover the Creator's Purpose for Men.* Ada, MI: Chosen Books, 2000.

Prince, Derek. *Marriage Covenant: The Biblical Secret for a Love That Lasts.* Springdale, PA: Whitaker House, 2000.

Recommended Books on Israel

Goll, James. *The Coming Israel Awakening: Gazing Into the Future of the Jewish People and the Church*, USA: Chosen Books, 2009.

McCarl, Jay. *The Best Day of Forever: Jesus, A Galilean Wedding And The End Of The World*, USA: Biblical Dinners Publishing, 2012.

Recommended Reading

In this appendix, we would like to comment further on some of the books already listed in the Selected Bibliography above, which have been particularly helpful to us on our journey to marriage. We have also recommended some additional books for those of you who might be interested in learning more about Israel, Jesus' return, and a Jewish understanding of End Times.

Books about Marriage

(Sarah writes): The three stand-out books for me were *The Power of a Praying Wife* by Stormie Omartian, *The First 90 Days of Marriage* by Eric Ludy and *Love & Respect* by Emerson Eggerichs.

The Power of a Praying Wife highlighted the value of praying for your husband. Only God can change the heart of your man and we can't make our husbands change, no matter how hard we try. This book got me started on praying for my future husband.

The book *The First 90 Days of Marriage* taught me about understanding your future spouse and working together through your differences. The author also stressed the importance of letting God be the author of your story. The term used was 'give God the pen' – in other words, let Him arrange how you meet your future spouse and how He brings you together. This phrase sustained me during my years of waiting as I continued to seek the Lord's direction. It was this advice that allowed me to leave potential suitors in God's hand and allow Him to write the story of the marriage He had for me.

The book *Love & Respect* was especially helpful as it illuminated the difference between the needs of men and the needs of women. It showed how women have a deep desire and need to know that they are loved. While men appreciate knowing they are loved, ultimately, their greater need is to know that they are respected and honoured. We live in a society that disrespects men and tries to pull down male authority figures. This book taught me the importance of breaking this cultural trend, by speaking words of encouragement to men in their God-given roles.

(Enoch writes): Although the aisles of Christian bookstores are full of books offering relationship advice, I was looking for advice that would be solidly founded on Scripture. The two books that helped me the most during this journey were *God is a Matchmaker* and *Husbands & Fathers* by Derek Prince.

In *God is a Matchmaker*, Derek shares the fascinating story about how God supernaturally led him into marriage to his first wife, Lydia, and later to his second wife, Ruth, after Lydia's death. His book lays out a solid Scriptural foundation for God's heart for marriage and the roles of husbands and wives.

At the time, one of Derek's conclusions in the book puzzled me. He believes that the biblical pattern, based on Adam and Eve, is that God is a matchmaker and that He does this by leading the right woman across the path of her future mate. I had always thought I should be out looking for my wife-to-be and was surprised to learn that God would simply lead my future wife across my path without my active intervention. The way it turned out, my marriage also followed the same principle. But had I embraced this principle earlier and truly rested in waiting for God to move, then it might have saved me lots of heartache.

Derek's book *Husbands and Fathers* also remains a favourite of mine because he eloquently and tenderly teaches men about the Father-heart of God while preparing them for their roles in their future families. I highly recommend this book.

Books About Israel and End Times

The Best Day of Forever: Jesus, A Galilean Wedding And The End Of The World by Jay McCarl is one of my all-time favourites. This amazing little book uncovers a wealth of information about ancient Jewish wedding traditions while applying it to our lives today.

The Coming Israel Awakening: Gazing Into the Future of the Jewish People and the Church by James Goll was the book that sparked my interest regarding Israel. It traces the history of modern Israel with a special focus on the miraculous work that God is doing in this nation today.

Other Books by the Author

In *The Jubilee: Discover The End Time Mystery*, join Ps Enoch Lavender as he uncovers key elements of the End Times from a fresh Messianic Perspective. The message of the Jubilee offers an exciting and uplifting perspective on the End Times through its original Jewish context. The Apostle Peter speaks of the Jubilee as "the restoration of all things... spoken by mouth of all His holy prophets" (Acts 3:21). In this book we are going to discover that the Jubilee offers a message of hope in the midst of darkness, of new life out of death, of entering one's God-given inheritance, of the wicked being deposed from power and the meek entering the Kingdom.

The Jubilee is available for order via Amazon, major Christian retailers as well as via www.olivetreeministries.tv

Other Books by the Author

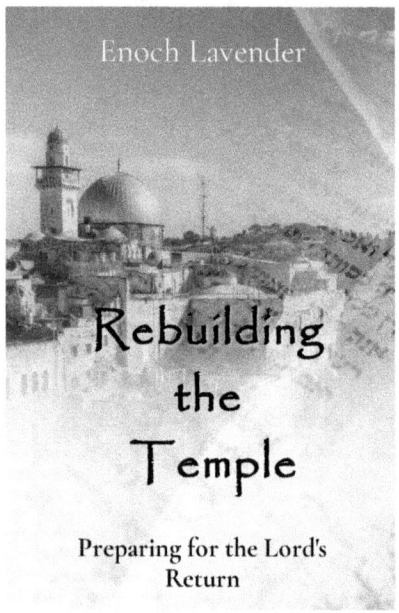

Rebuilding the Temple: Preparing for the Lord's Return chronicles recent developments regarding the Third Temple in light of its key role in Bible Prophecy.

In this book, Ps. Enoch Lavender examines the challenging topic of the Abomination of Desolation as well as the surprising potential role of Islam in the rebuilding of the Temple. *Rebuilding the Temple* examines the miracles of the 6 Day War, the recent and unexpected rise of a Temple Mount advocate to Israel's national stage, and the reasons why the Temple – despite many obstacles – will one day be built.

Book available for order via Amazon, major Christian retailers as well as via www.olivetreeministries.tv

About the Author

Ps Enoch Lavender writes regular articles about current events as they relate to Bible Prophecy and is a regular contributor to Christian newspapers, magazines and web sites in the US, UK, Australia and New Zealand.

Enoch's teaching programs can been seen on TBN pacific and on Becoming Greater TV. In addition, Enoch hosts a popular YouTube channel with a growing international following and featuring over 100 of his teaching messages.

Enoch has been studying Hebrew and the Jewish origins of Christianity for the past 10 years and is based with his wife and three kids in Northern NSW, Australia.

Visit our ministry web site for in depth teaching articles and videos on related topics as well as a resource store.

www.olivetreeministries.tv.

Speaking Engagements

We would love the opportunity to share our story with your church or youth group. To discuss further, please contact us via either of our web site.

www.ingramcontent.com/pod-product-compliance
Lightning Source LLC
Chambersburg PA
CBHW071412290426
44108CB00014B/1787